Virtual Tax

Virtual Tax: The taxation of virtual currency

Published by Desert Mystery Publishing, LLC

2020 edition published October 2019
Revised August 2020

Cover art: Mariah Wall
Book layout by Paper Crane Books

Virtual Tax:
The taxation of virtual currency

2020 Edition

by Amy M. Wall, EA, MBA

For Mona Coury, the Tax Goddess

Important Notice:

Tax law as it pertains to virtual currency is very much in its infancy. This book is designed to provide information on the taxation of virtual currency—to the best of the author's understanding—as of the date of publication. Future guidance from the IRS is needed to clarify many issues.

For this reason, the author and publisher do not guarantee or warrant any information contained herein: competent professional advice should always be sought for your particular situation.

Further, the author and publisher are not engaged in legal services, and no information contained herein should be construed as legal advice. As an IRS Circular 230 practitioner, I have no responsibility for any positions you take on your tax return, unless I have prepared and signed that tax return. For detailed analysis of your tax situation, please consult your tax advisor.

If you need assistance with virtual currency taxes, you can contact me directly at amy@tucsontaxteam.com. I work with virtual currency users and tax practitioners all over the country.

Table of Contents

Preface

THIS NEW EDITION OF *VIRTUAL TAX* includes background on virtual currency that can help tax professionals get more comfortable dealing with this subject. If you're already a miner, trader, etc., feel free to skip the first section of this book. You probably know more than I do.

From a tax standpoint, the difficulty presented by virtual currency is simply this: it's often used as a currency, and is even called currency, but it's taxed as property. Because it is taxed as property, there are taxable gains and losses upon sale. Because it is also used as currency, purchases and sales occur frequently and often in micro amounts. This is a new type of asset that all of us in Tax World are struggling to get our (virtual) arms around.

1
Virtual Currency

FIRST, LET'S UNDERSTAND THAT THERE are differences between digital currency, virtual currency, and cryptocurrency.

If you Google these terms, you'll find different definitions presented by different people but, basically, digital currency is just what you think it is: currency that is stored and transferred electronically. Most money in the world is digital currency. Your debit card could be considered digital. For that matter, your bank account is probably digital as well. Your bank certainly doesn't have all its customers' money sitting in a vault onsite.

Virtual currency is a type of digital currency that is controlled by its creators and may be used for payment among members of a particular virtual community. This type of currency has no central point of regulation—no bank, no credit card agency, no broker—and, though it may be used by natural or legal persons as a means of exchange, virtual currency does not possess the status of legal tender; it is not a fiat currency.

Cryptocurrency is a subset of virtual currency; it refers to a type of virtual currency that utilizes encryption algorithms and techniques to ensure security. Bitcoin, Ether, Litecoin, etc., are cryptocurrencies.

(Note: Because the IRS uses the term virtual currency to denote both virtual and crypto currencies, I'm following that precedent throughout this book.)

People who aren't familiar with virtual currency often ask, "What problems are virtual and cryptocurrencies trying to solve? Why is this even a thing?"

It's a thing because many people see that virtual currency has the potential to solve a significant money problem.

Money has always had its problems. Back in the bartering days, the problem was finding someone who had something you wanted and also wanted something that you had. If I had lots of strawberries but no bread, then my goal would be to find someone who had lots of bread, but no strawberries. Clearly a problem.

Then there were some goods that were fairly easily traded without requiring direct barter: salt, animal skins, weapons, etc. The problem at that point was one of transportation, as these items took up physical space and had to be moved from place to place.

There were some early currencies in the form of metal coins. The first minted currency was that of a country called Lydia (an Iron Age kingdom in the area of Turkey) in 600 BC. These coins were a mixture of silver and gold and were minted in different denominations.

The Chinese then took it to the next level with paper money during the Tang Dynasty. Interesting tidbit: American bills say, "In God We Trust"; the Chinese bills said, "All counterfeiters will be decapitated." Serious stuff.

The first paper currency used in Europe was printed in Sweden in 1601. The first paper money in America was issued by the Massachusetts Bay Colony in 1690 to finance a military expedition to Canada.

Paper money was distrusted for a long time (much as virtual currency is distrusted now); the gold standard helped citizens overcome that distrust. The gold standard meant that the government would redeem paper money for its value in gold. The Federal Reserve was created in 1913 to stabilize gold and currency values. By 1970, the US no longer held enough gold to cover all the dollar holdings in the world; President Nixon took the US off the gold standard in August of 1971. As of that time, money's value was perceived, rather than actual; money became a *concept*, rather than a *thing*.

The problem with paper or metal currencies in a global economy is, again, transportation. How do I pay someone who isn't sitting in front of me?

Thus, credit cards. Credit cards originated with Diners Club in 1950, and were used mainly for travel and entertainment. American Express was launched in 1958 and introduced the first plastic (rather than paper) card. From there, we've gone to mobile payment systems.

We no longer have a problem with paying long

distance; instead we have another problem. If you want to pay someone who isn't sitting in front of you holding their hand out for cash, you need a third party. Every time. EVERY. TIME. You need a bank to process the debit card transaction. Or you need a credit card processor to handle the credit card payment. Or you need Paypal. There's literally no way to pay someone who isn't sitting in front of you with their hand out unless you have a third party facilitating the transaction. And this wouldn't be much of a problem, except that this third party has to be paid for their services.

Can you imagine how much money is poured into the waiting hands of banks, credit card processors, etc.? I recently saw an estimate of $42.4 billion dollars collected from vendors by credit card companies in 2016. That's BILLIONS of dollars.

So—goes the thinking—what if we could do without that third party? What if there was a way to process payments that didn't involve cash and didn't involve third parties sucking up billions of dollars? Wouldn't that be a good thing?

This idea is called "decentralizing" . . . and thus, virtual currency was born.

In November 1998 a computer engineer named Wei Dai published an essay proposing an anonymous, distributed electronic cash system called B-money.

In 2005, a computer scientist and cryptographer named Nick Szabo proposed a decentralized financial system incorporating time-stamped blocks and proof-of-work strings; the result would be secure storage and transferring. He called it "Bit Gold".

In 2009, an unknown person or persons named Nakamoto authored a paper on Bitcoin and devised the first blockchain database. Bitcoin is a decentralized currency (so no bank or credit card processing agencies). It utilizes a distributed ledger, meaning that the "books", as it were, are open and available to anyone on the system. (Understand here that the names of users aren't on the ledger; what is seen is just the relevant information about the transaction such as the amount, date, etc.)

With a distributed ledger all transaction histories are stored and updated continuously, constantly, reliably. The data relevant to each transaction is stored in a data string called a "blockchain", which is completely secure and unalterable.

The idea of a secure data string has many possibilities outside the creation of virtual currency. The blockchain is considered by many people to be the biggest modern revolution since the internet.

The first Bitcoin transaction, now famous, occurred in 2010 when programmer Laszlo Hanyecz purchased two Papa John's pizzas for 10,000 BTC (Bitcoins).

Since that time, more than 4,000 types of "altcoins" (coins other than Bitcoin) have been created. The tax preparer doesn't need to know much about them, other than that they exist.

2
GAO Report of May 2013

ISSUES CONCERNING THE TAXATION OF virtual currency were first addressed in May of 2013 by the United States Government Accountability Office in a report to the Committee on Finance, U.S. Senate. It was called "Virtual Economies and Currencies: Additional IRS Guidance Could Reduce Tax Compliance Risks".

It's enjoyable reading, particularly since the Report is far more interested in MMORPGs (Massively Multiplayer Online Role-Playing Games) than in Bitcoin. I discuss the tax implications of MMORPGs in Chapter 21.

The Report defined virtual currency as "...generally, a digital unit of exchange that is not backed by a government-issued legal tender. Virtual currencies can be used entirely within a virtual economy or can be used in lieu of a government-issued currency to purchase goods and services in the real economy." I guess that's as good a definition as any.

The Report laid out a case for taxable transactions

resulting from the use of virtual currency in or out of the context of virtual economies such as MMORPGs. It stated that there are tax compliance risks involved with virtual currency and virtual economics, specifically taxpayers' lack of knowledge about the tax requirements; uncertainty over how to characterize income; uncertainty over how to calculate basis (more detail on that later) for gains; challenges with third-party reporting (the lack thereof); and tax evasion.

Bottom line? Taxpayers don't know how to report their virtual currency income, and might not want to, even if they did know how. (Which sounds pretty much like the so-called real economy, come to think of it.) Further, as the use of virtual currencies and virtual economies grows, the risk of tax noncompliance grows as well.

The Report acknowledged that back in 2007 the IRS had identified and surveyed various information sources relative to virtual economics but had ultimately decided that the amount of lost revenue did not justify taking resources away from higher priority needs. In 2009, the IRS went so far as to put guidance online regarding virtual economy transactions. (I have yet to find this online guidance; presumably it's been taken down.) The Report then called the IRS out for not having issued guidance specific to virtual currencies outside of virtual economies and suggested that the IRS find relatively low-cost ways to provide information to taxpayers.

3
Notice 2014-21

THE IRS RESPONDED A YEAR LATER, on March 15, 2014, by issuing a whopping, no-expense-spared, six pages of guidance in the form of Notice 2014-21. A Notice is usually issued prior to being officially published in the Internal Revenue Bulletin; the Bulletin is the ultimate authority and the Notice is simply a preview of what's going into the Internal Revenue Bulletin. So yes, the Notice is official IRS guidance.

Let's read through the Notice together to make sure we understand the important points. The text of the Notice is quoted verbatim and is indented; my comments are shown in bold type.

Section 1. Purpose

This notice describes how existing general tax principles apply to transactions using virtual currency. The notice provides this guidance in the form of answers to frequently asked questions.

Section 2. Background

The Internal Revenue Service (IRS) is aware that "virtual currency" may be used to pay for goods or services, or held for investment. Virtual currency is a digital representation of value that functions as a medium of exchange, a unit of account, and/or a store of value. In some environments, it operates like "real" currency—i.e., the coin and paper money of the United States or of any other country that is designated as legal tender, circulates, and is customarily used and accepted as a medium of exchange in the country of issuance—but it does not have legal tender status in any jurisdiction.

Virtual currency that has an equivalent value in real currency, or that acts as a substitute for real currency, is referred to as "convertible" virtual currency. Bitcoin is one example of a convertible virtual currency. Bitcoin can be digitally traded between users and can be purchased for, or exchanged into, U.S. dollars, Euros, and other real or virtual currencies. For a more comprehensive description of convertible virtual currencies to date, see Financial Crimes Enforcement Network (FinCEN) *Guidance on the Application of FinCEN's Regulations to Persons Administering, Exchanging, or Using Virtual Currencies* (FIN-2013-G001, March 18, 2013).

Section 3. Scope

In general, the sale or exchange of convertible virtual currency, or the use of convertible virtual currency to pay for goods or services in a real-world economy transaction, has tax consequences that may result in a tax liability. This notice addresses only the U.S. federal tax consequences of transactions in, or transactions that use, convertible virtual currency, and the term "virtual currency" as used in Section 4 refers only to convertible virtual currency.

No inference should be drawn with respect to virtual currencies not described in this notice. The Treasury Department and the IRS recognize that there may be other questions regarding the tax consequences of virtual currency not addressed in this notice that warrant consideration. Therefore, the Treasury Department and the IRS request comments from the public regarding other types or aspects of virtual currency transactions that should be addressed in future guidance.

For purposes of the FAQs in this notice, the taxpayer's functional currency is assumed to be the U.S. dollar, the taxpayer is assumed to use the cash receipts and disbursements method of accounting and the taxpayer is assumed not to be under common control with any other party to a transaction.

OK, so far, so good. The IRS recognizes the existence of virtual currency, and that it may be used to purchase "real world" goods and services. The Notice makes an important distinction between convertible virtual currencies (meaning currencies that may be utilized in place of fiat currency) as opposed to a virtual currency that may not be so utilized.

Section 4. Frequently Asked Questions

Q-1: How is virtual currency treated for federal tax purposes?

A-1: For federal tax purposes, virtual currency is treated as property. General tax principles applicable to property transactions apply to transactions using virtual currency.

This is the single most important statement in the Notice. For the tax-savvy, all the rest is just commentary. Defining virtual currency as property means that every time virtual currency is spent, sold, traded, exchanged, gifted, donated, inherited or even lost, a potential taxable event has taken place. For virtual currency users, defining virtual currency as property was a devastating blow.

Q-2: Is virtual currency treated as currency for purposes of determining whether a transaction results in foreign currency gain or loss under U.S. federal tax laws?

A-2: No. Under currently applicable law, virtual currency is not treated as currency that could generate foreign currency gain or loss for U.S. federal tax purposes.

More bad news. Foreign currency gain has a de minimis of $200, meaning that if you have a gain of less than $200 you don't have to bother reporting it. No such luck with virtual currency.

Q-3: Must a taxpayer who receives virtual currency as payment for goods or services include in computing gross income the fair market value of the virtual currency?

A-3: Yes. A taxpayer who receives virtual currency as payment for goods or services must, in computing gross income, include the fair market value of the virtual currency, measured in U.S. dollars, as of the date that the virtual currency was received. See Publication 525, Taxable and Nontaxable Income, for more information on miscellaneous income from exchanges involving property or services.

This was obvious as soon as the Notice said the word "property". Of course, anytime you receive property in exchange for goods and services, you have income. Out in the "real" world, this is called barter income: I'll do your bookkeeping in exchange for you painting my house. Both sides have reportable income which, as dutiful US citizens, they have reported on their tax returns.

> **Q-4:** What is the basis of virtual currency received as payment for goods or services in Q&A-3?

> **A-4:** The basis of virtual currency that a taxpayer receives as payment for goods or services in Q&A-3 is the fair market value of the virtual currency in U.S. dollars as of the date of receipt. See Publication 551, Basis of Assets, for more information on the computation of basis when property is received for goods or services.

The term "basis" is familiar to tax geeks, but not so much to normal people. Basis, essentially, is what something is worth in Tax World. If you buy stock for $100, then your basis in the stock is $100. If you buy a car for $1,500, then that car's basis is $1,500. If you add leather seats for $200, then the car's basis is now $1,700. Don't be fooled by these simplistic examples; basis is actually a complex tax topic. The reason basis is important is that it determines your gain or loss when you dispose of property. So, just as with any other property, your basis in the virtual currency is, generally speaking, the fair market value of that currency as of the date you received it. More—much more—on this later.

Q-5: How is the fair market value of virtual currency determined?

A-5: For U.S. tax purposes, transactions using virtual currency must be reported in U.S. dollars. Therefore, taxpayers will be required to determine the fair market value of virtual currency in U.S. dollars as of the date of payment or receipt. If a virtual currency is listed on an exchange and the exchange rate is established by market supply and demand, the fair market value of the virtual currency is determined by converting the virtual currency into U.S. dollars (or into another real currency which in turn can be converted into U.S. dollars) at the exchange rate, in a reasonable manner that is consistently applied.

How is that fair market value determined? Easily: just look up the price as of that date on your blockchain explorer. Not hard.

Q-6: Does a taxpayer have gain or loss upon an exchange of virtual currency for other property?

A-6: Yes. If the fair market value of property received in exchange for virtual currency exceeds the taxpayer's adjusted basis of the virtual currency, the taxpayer has taxable gain. The taxpayer has a loss if the fair market value of the property received is less than the adjusted basis of the virtual currency. See Publication 544, Sales and Other Dispositions of Assets, for information about the tax treatment of sales and exchanges, such as whether a loss is deductible.

The rubber meets the road here. When you exchange virtual currency for other property, you have effectively sold it. You take the value of that currency on the date you exchanged it (yes, look it up on a blockchain explorer) and subtract your basis. If the remaining number is positive (it was worth more on the day you exchanged it than on the day you earned it), you have a gain. If it is negative (it was worth more on the day you earned it than on the day you exchanged it), you have a loss.

Q-7: What type of gain or loss does a taxpayer realize on the sale or exchange of virtual currency?

A-7: The character of the gain or loss generally depends on whether the virtual currency is a capital asset in the hands of the taxpayer. A taxpayer generally realizes capital gain or loss on the sale or exchange of virtual currency that is a capital asset in the hands of the taxpayer. For example, stocks, bonds, and other investment property are generally capital assets. A taxpayer generally realizes ordinary gain or loss on the sale or exchange of virtual currency that is not a capital asset in the hands of the taxpayer. Inventory and other property held mainly for sale to customers in a trade or business are examples of property that is not a capital asset. See Publication 544 for more information about capital assets and the character of gain or loss.

Now it's getting a little complex. For most people, this all translates as "long-term if I owned it for 366 days or more" and "short-term if I owned it for less than 366 days". If you are a money service business and actually do have virtual currency that you are selling to others, then the virtual currency is treated as inventory and your income is going to be ordinary income/losses, not capital gains/losses.

If your virtual currency is used for personal purchases, then you'll have to report any gains, but you might not get to take losses. I say "might not" because losses on personal property aren't deductible. So if the

IRS decides that virtual currency held in an account that is also used for personal purchases is considered personal property, gains are taxable, but losses aren't allowed. And this would be bad. More on this later.

Q-8: Does a taxpayer who "mines" virtual currency (for example, uses computer resources to validate Bitcoin transactions and maintain the public Bitcoin transaction ledger) realize gross income upon receipt of the virtual currency resulting from those activities?

A-8: Yes, when a taxpayer successfully "mines" virtual currency, the fair market value of the virtual currency as of the date of receipt is includible in gross income. See Publication 525, Taxable and Nontaxable Income, for more information on taxable income.

Mining is, of course, the process by which virtual currency is born. Or created. Or released. Whatever. It's income. But what type of income? Read on.

Q-9: Is an individual who "mines" virtual currency as a trade or business subject to self-employment tax on the income derived from those activities?

A-9: If a taxpayer's "mining" of virtual currency constitutes a trade or business, and the "mining" activity is not undertaken by the taxpayer as an employee, the net earnings from self-employment (generally, gross income derived from carrying on a trade or business less allowable deductions) resulting from those activities constitute self-employment income and are subject to the self-employment tax. See Chapter 10 of Publication 334, *Tax Guide for Small Business*, for more information on self-employment tax and Publication 535, *Business Expenses*, for more information on determining whether expenses are from a business activity carried on to make a profit.

Not just any old income; it's self-employment income. Why is this important? Because self-employment income gets its own special tax called FICA tax (aka Social Security and Medicare aka Self-Employment Tax). FICA tax runs about 15.3% of the net gain. This is in addition to regular Federal and State income tax.

Q-10: Does virtual currency received by an independent contractor for performing services constitute self-employment income?

A-10: Yes. Generally, self-employment income includes all gross income derived by an individual from any trade or business carried on by the individual as other than an employee. Consequently, the fair market value of virtual currency received for services performed as an independent contractor, measured in U.S. dollars as of the date of receipt, constitutes self-employment income and is subject to the self-employment tax. See FS-2007-18, April 2007, *Business or Hobby? Answer Has Implications for Deductions*, for information on determining whether an activity is a business or a hobby.

Just in case you hadn't figured this part out, if you are an independent contractor and you are being paid in virtual currency, this is taxable income. And, yes, it is also subject to FICA tax (aka Social Security and Medicare aka Self-Employment Tax).

Q-11: Does virtual currency paid by an employer as remuneration for services constitute wages for employment tax purposes?

A-11: Yes. Generally, the medium in which remuneration for services is paid is immaterial to the determination of whether the remuneration constitutes wages for employment tax purposes. Consequently, the fair market value of virtual currency paid as wages is subject to federal income tax withholding, Federal Insurance Contributions

Act (FICA) tax, and Federal Unemployment Tax Act (FUTA) tax and must be reported on Form W-2, *Wage and Tax Statement*. See Publication 15 (Circular E), *Employer's Tax Guide*, for information on the withholding, depositing, reporting, and paying of employment taxes.

If your employer pays you wages in virtual currency, this is taxed just like regular wages. Again, no different from how you'd report the receipt of any other type of property. If your employer paid you with a 1967 Chevy, the fair market value of that Chevy as of the date you received it would be part of your pay. And yes, the employer must withhold FICA taxes on that fair market value.

Q-12: Is a payment made using virtual currency subject to information reporting?

A-12: A payment made using virtual currency is subject to information reporting to the same extent as any other payment made in property. For example, a person who in the course of a trade or business makes a payment of fixed and determinable income using virtual currency with a value of $600 or more to a U.S. non-exempt recipient in a taxable year is required to report the payment to the IRS and to the payee. Examples of payments of fixed and determinable income include rent, salaries, wages, premiums, annuities, and compensation.

Q-13: Is a person who in the course of a trade or business makes a payment using virtual currency worth $600 or more to an independent contractor for performing services required to file an information return with the IRS?

A-13: Generally, a person who in the course of a trade or business makes a payment of $600 or more in a taxable year to an independent contractor for the performance of services is required to report that payment to the IRS and to the payee on Form 1099-MISC, *Miscellaneous Income.* Payments of virtual currency required to be reported on Form 1099-MISC should be reported using the fair market value of the virtual currency in U.S. dollars as of the date of payment. The payment recipient may have income even if the recipient does not receive a Form 1099-MISC. See the Instructions to Form 1099-MISC and the General Instructions for Certain Information Returns for more information. For payments to non-U.S. persons, see Publication 515, *Withholding of Tax on Nonresident Aliens and Foreign Entities.*

If, in the course of your business, you pay someone with virtual currency that is worth $600 or more at the time it was paid, then you are required to send a 1099-MISC to that person and to the IRS. This isn't new: you are required to send a 1099-MISC anytime your business pays a non-corporation $600 or more in a calendar year.

Q-14: Are payments made using virtual currency subject to backup withholding?

A-14: Payments made using virtual currency are subject to backup withholding to the same extent as other payments made in property. Therefore, payors making reportable payments using virtual currency must solicit a taxpayer identification number (TIN) from the payee. The payor must backup withhold from the payment if a TIN is not obtained prior to payment or if the payor receives notification from the IRS that backup withholding is required. See Publication 1281, *Backup Withholding for Missing and Incorrect Name/TINs*, for more information.

The point being made over and over here is that there is no escape from any tax or reporting requirement just because payment is made in virtual currency rather than US dollars. You still have to pay tax, you still have to withhold FICA, you still have to send in 1099s, and if

the person you paid didn't give you a tax identification number, you still have to do back up withholding.

Q-15: Are there IRS information reporting requirements for a person who settles payments made in virtual currency on behalf of merchants that accept virtual currency from their customers?

A-15: Yes, if certain requirements are met. In general, a third party that contracts with a substantial number of unrelated merchants to settle payments between the merchants and their customers is a third-party settlement organization (TPSO). A TPSO is required to report payments made to a merchant on a Form 1099-K, *Payment Card and Third Party Network Transactions*, if, for the calendar year, both (1) the number of transactions settled for the merchant exceeds 200, and (2) the gross amount of payments made to the merchant exceeds $20,000. When completing Boxes 1, 3, and 5a-1 on the Form 1099-K, transactions where the TPSO settles payments made with virtual currency are aggregated with transactions where the TPSO settles payments made with real currency to determine the total amounts to be reported in those boxes. When determining whether the transactions are reportable, the value of the virtual currency is the fair market value of the virtual currency in

U.S. dollars on the date of payment. See The Third Party Information Reporting Center, http://www.irs.gov/TaxProfessionals/Third-Party-Reporting-Information-Center, for more information on reporting transactions on Form 1099-K.

Virtual currency transactions are often settled by credit card. If you have traded a lot of virtual currency during a calendar year, you may very well get a K-1 from the credit card company showing the total that was paid to your credit card during that year. Heads up: the same statement was sent to the IRS, and that gross amount better show up in your tax return somewhere.

Q-16: Will taxpayers be subject to penalties for having treated a virtual currency transaction in a manner that is inconsistent with this notice prior to March 25, 2014?

A-16: Taxpayers may be subject to penalties for failure to comply with tax laws. For example, underpayments attributable to virtual currency transactions may be subject to penalties, such as accuracy-related penalties under §6662. In addition, failure to timely or correctly report virtual currency transactions when required to do so may be subject to information reporting penalties under §6721 and §6722. However, penalty relief may be available to taxpayers and persons required to file an information return who are able to establish that the underpayment or failure to properly file information returns is due to reasonable cause.

And here's the really fun part: just because the IRS didn't tell you sooner what the tax requirements were doesn't mean that you are exempt from those tax requirements. You may need to amend past year tax returns in order to stay compliant with tax law and you may get hit with penalties.

Section 5. Drafting Information

The principal author of this notice is Keith A. Aqui of the Office of Associate Chief Counsel (Income Tax & Accounting). For further information about income tax issues addressed in this notice, please contact Mr. Aqui at (202) 317-4718; for further information about employment tax issues addressed in this notice, please contact Mr. Neil D. Shepherd at (202) 317-4774; for further information about information reporting issues addressed in this notice, please contact Ms. Adrienne E. Griffin at (202) 317-6845; and for further information regarding foreign currency issues addressed in this notice, please contact Mr. Raymond J. Stahl at (202) 317-6938. These are not toll-free calls.

Here's a quick and dirty summation of what you just read: Virtual currency is property. Payment received as virtual currency must be included as taxable income; to determine the amount of income to include, convert the virtual currency received to dollars using the fair market value of that virtual currency on the date of receipt. The character of gain or loss depends on the character of the virtual currency in the hands of the taxpayer. Mining of virtual currency creates income for the miner—again, at the fair market value of the currency on the date of receipt. Further, mining constitutes a trade or business and is thus subject to self-employment tax; virtual currency received by an independent contractor in exchange for goods and services is also subject to self-employment tax. The reporting and back-up withholding required of an employer or other payee who pays in US dollars is also required of an employer or other payee who pays in virtual currency. Taxpayers who did not comply with the requirements of this notice prior to its date of issue may be subject to penalties.

4
IRS Notice 2019-24

FIVE YEARS LATER, the IRS issued Notice 2019-24 to answer some of the outstanding issues surrounding the taxation of virtual currency. Again, this Notice is official IRS guidance.

Following is the text of the Notice, indented, with my comments shown in bold type.

Issues

(1) Does a taxpayer have gross income under § 61 of the Internal Revenue Code (Code) as a result of a hard fork of a cryptocurrency the taxpayer owns if the taxpayer does not receive units of a new cryptocurrency?

(2) Does a taxpayer have gross income under § 61 as a result of an airdrop of a new cryptocurrency following a hard fork if the taxpayer receives units of new cryptocurrency?

Background

Virtual currency is a digital representation of value that functions as a medium of exchange, a unit of account, and a store of value other than a representation of the United States dollar or a foreign currency. Foreign currency is the coin and paper money of a country other than the United States that is designated as legal tender, circulates, and is customarily used and accepted as a medium of exchange in the country of issuance. See 31 C.F.R. § 1010.100(m).

Cryptocurrency is a type of virtual currency that utilizes cryptography to secure transactions that are digitally recorded on a distributed ledger, such as a blockchain. Units of cryptocurrency are generally referred to as coins or tokens. Distributed ledger technology uses independent digital systems to record, share, and synchronize transactions, the details of which are recorded in multiple places at the same time with no central data store or administration functionality.

A hard fork is unique to distributed ledger technology and occurs when a cryptocurrency on a distributed ledger undergoes a protocol change resulting in a permanent diversion from the legacy or existing distributed ledger. A hard fork may result in the creation of a new cryptocurrency on a new distributed ledger in addition to the legacy cryptocurrency on the legacy distributed ledger. Following a hard fork, transactions involving the new cryptocurrency are recorded on the new distributed ledger and transactions involving the legacy cryptocurrency continue to be recorded on the legacy distributed ledger.

An airdrop is a means of distributing units of a cryptocurrency to the distributed ledger addresses of multiple taxpayers. A hard fork followed by an airdrop results in the distribution of units of the new cryptocurrency to addresses containing the legacy cryptocurrency. However, a hard fork is not always followed by an airdrop.

Cryptocurrency from an airdrop generally is received on the date and at the time it is recorded on the distributed ledger. However, a taxpayer may constructively receive cryptocurrency prior to the airdrop being recorded on the distributed ledger. A taxpayer does not have receipt of cryptocurrency when the airdrop is recorded on the distributed ledger if the taxpayer is not able to exercise dominion and control over the cryptocurrency. For example, a taxpayer does not have dominion and control if the address to which the cryptocurrency is airdropped is contained in a wallet managed through a cryptocurrency exchange and the cryptocurrency exchange does not support the newly-created cryptocurrency such that the airdropped cryptocurrency is not immediately credited to the taxpayer's account at the cryptocurrency exchange. If the taxpayer later acquires the ability to transfer, sell, exchange, or otherwise dispose of the cryptocurrency, the taxpayer is treated as receiving the cryptocurrency at that time.

The IRS here defines forks and airdrops, and clarifies the fact that currency is only constructively received when the taxpayer is able to access that currency.

Facts

Situation 1: A holds 50 units of Crypto M, a cryptocurrency. On Date 1, the distributed ledger for Crypto M experiences a hard fork, resulting in the creation of Crypto N. Crypto N is not airdropped or otherwise transferred to an account owned or controlled by A.

Situation 2: B holds 50 units of Crypto R, a cryptocurrency. On Date 2, the distributed ledger for Crypto R experiences a hard fork, resulting in the creation of Crypto S. On that date, 25 units of Crypto S are airdropped to B's distributed ledger address and B has the ability to dispose of Crypto S immediately following the airdrop. B now holds

50 units of Crypto R and 25 units of Crypto S. The airdrop of Crypto S is recorded on the distributed ledger on Date 2 at Time 1 and, at that date and time, the fair market value of B's 25 units of Crypto S is $50. B receives the Crypto S solely because B owns Crypto R at the time of the hard fork. After the airdrop, transactions involving Crypto S are recorded on the new distributed ledger and transactions involving Crypto R continue to be recorded on the legacy distributed ledger.

Law And Analysis

Section 61(a)(3) provides that, except as otherwise provided by law, gross income means all income from whatever source derived, including gains from dealings in property. Under § 61, all gains or undeniable accessions to wealth, clearly realized, over which a taxpayer has complete dominion, are included in gross income. See Commissioner v. Glenshaw Glass Co., 348 U.S. 426, 431 (1955). In general, income is ordinary unless it is gain from the sale or exchange of a capital asset or a special rule applies. See, e.g., §§ 1222, 1231, 1234A.

Section 1011 of the Code provides that a taxpayer's adjusted basis for determining the gain or loss from the sale or exchange of property is the cost or other basis determined under § 1012 of the Code, adjusted to the extent provided under § 1016 of the Code. When a taxpayer receives property that is not purchased, unless otherwise provided in the Code, the taxpayer's basis in the property received is determined by reference to the amount included in gross income, which is the fair market value of the property when the property is received. See generally §§ 61 and 1011; see also § 1.61-2(d)(2)(i).

Section 451 of the Code provides that a taxpayer using the cash method of accounting includes an amount in gross income in the taxable year it is actually or constructively received. See §§ 1.451-1 and 1.451-2. A taxpayer using an accrual method of accounting generally includes an amount in gross income no later than the taxable year in which all the events have occurred which fix the right to receive such amount. See § 451.

Situation 1: A did not receive units of the new cryptocurrency, Crypto N, from the hard fork; therefore, A does not have an accession to wealth and does not have gross income under § 61 as a result of the hard fork.

Situation 2: B received a new asset, Crypto S, in the airdrop following the hard fork; therefore, B has an accession to wealth and has ordinary income in the taxable year in which the Crypto S is received. See §§ 61 and 451. B has dominion and control of Crypto S at the time of the airdrop, when it is recorded on the distributed ledger, because B immediately has the ability to dispose of Crypto S. The amount included in gross income is $50, the fair market value of B's 25 units of Crypto S when the airdrop is recorded on the distributed ledger. B's basis in Crypto S is $50, the amount of income recognized. See §§ 61, 1011, and 1.61-2(d)(2)(i).

Here we learn that the amount of income to be reported is the fair market value of that new currency as of the date received. The problem with this, of course, is that the fair market value of this currency may not be easily determined as of that date; you'll have to do the best you can to determine and document the fair market value as soon as possible after receipt.

That fair market value then becomes your basis in that currency, and you'll have a capital gain or loss when you sell this currency. The income to be reported is ordinary income, not a capital gain.

Note this means that a third party can create income for you without your knowledge or consent, simply by forking a network or creating an airdrop.

Holdings

(1) A taxpayer does not have gross income under § 61 as a result of a hard fork of a cryptocurrency the taxpayer owns if the taxpayer does not receive units of a new cryptocurrency. (2) A taxpayer has gross income, ordinary in character, under § 61 as a result of an airdrop of a new cryptocurrency following a hard fork if the taxpayer receives units of new cryptocurrency.

Drafting Information

The principal author of this revenue ruling is Suzanne R. Sinno of the Office of Associate Chief Counsel (Income Tax & Accounting). For further information regarding the revenue ruling, contact Ms. Sinno at (202) 317-4718 (not a toll-free number).

This Notice does not have a retroactive statement, so *presumably* tax returns filed prior to 2019 *possibly* are not required to abide by it. *Presumably*, then, those who chose, in earlier years, to not report income on their forked or airdropped currency now have a zero basis in that currency moving forward. I emphasize *presumably* and *possibly* because the IRS has not commented on this situation.

5
Earning Virtual Currency

MOST PEOPLE WHO EARN VIRTUAL currency are treated as self-employed. These taxpayers file a Schedule C with their 1040 returns and bear the responsibility for paying their own Social Security and Medicare taxes as well as income taxes.

You are required by law to report income even if you have not received documentation such as a 1099-MISC or a W-2 from the person who hired you, and even if you received it in cash. (I'm not commenting on the likelihood of you getting caught if you don't report it; I'm stating the law of Tax World.)

If you function as a retail store or online business and you accept virtual currency as payment for the goods and services you provide, then you're responsible for translating that virtual currency into its dollar value and reporting it as income.

If you aren't sure whether or not you are self-employed the bottom line is this: if the person paying you virtual currency doesn't withhold Social Security and Medicare taxes for you (and does not generate a tax form at the end of the year to tell you how much they withheld) then paying these taxes is up to you. Employees get help in paying these taxes: their employer withholds 6.2% of their wages for Social security plus 1.45% for Medicare and then matches that amount, sending in a total of 12.4% for Social Security and 2.90% for Medicare. If you don't have an employer paying the other half, then you've got to pay that 15.3% tax all by yourself. When you add income tax to that 15.3%, you can owe quite a bit to the IRS when you file your return.

Your self-employment income is the dollar value of that money at the time of "constructive receipt". Constructive receipt is defined as that moment when the funds are available to the taxpayer without substantial limitations. If a check is available to you but you haven't cashed it, you have nonetheless constructively received it. If you must travel to Japan to get the money and you hadn't expected to have to make the trip at that time, then you might be considered not to have had constructive receipt until you actually made the trip and received the money. (But then you might have to prove that you hadn't expected to make the trip.)

The concept of constructive receipt is an important one in the world of virtual currency because the value of virtual currency can vary substantially. A dollar today is a dollar tomorrow, but a bitcoin today isn't likely to have the same dollar value as a bitcoin tomorrow.

Under the doctrine of constructive receipt, you have received income as soon as the virtual currency hits your wallet or becomes available to you in a similar way. Generally, the exchange you are using will give you the dollar value of that income upon receipt. If you don't have an exchange helping you out, then it becomes entirely your responsibility to determine the value of the received virtual currency, document how you calculated that value, and retain that documentation. It isn't the IRS' job to calculate the income you received; it's your job to figure that out and to prove the value of that income if asked to do so.

Remember that you are required to pay tax on any income you receive, whether or not you spend it. Even if you leave that virtual currency in your wallet for the next ten years, it's still considered taxable income upon receipt. When you do spend the virtual currency there's another taxable event—but let's not get too far ahead.

Of course, being self-employed means you can deduct ordinary and necessary business expenses from your income. If you work from your home, it's possible that you can deduct part of your home expenses as an office-in-home. If your work requires you to purchase equipment or software, you may be able to deduct those expenses. Typical expenses for the miner include computers, ASICs (application-specific integrated circuits), home office, and electricity. (Note to tax preparers: those ASICs usually don't have a useful life of more than one year so it's arguable that they should be expensed, not depreciated.)

Always retain documentation supporting those expenses; Schedule C is the single most audited form in all of Tax World.

Business expenses are similar for *all small businesses,* and your tax preparer should be able to explain what's deductible and what isn't, even if he or she isn't particularly familiar with virtual currency.

If you owe a substantial amount to the IRS and don't meet the requirements for exceptions, you will also have to pay an underpayment penalty plus interest on both the unpaid tax and the penalty. To avoid penalties and interest, you should make quarterly tax payments throughout the year or increase your federal withholding on income from other sources.

Be proactive: talk to your tax preparer about estimating your income and expenses so that you can make adequate estimated tax payments.

6
Paying with Virtual Currency

NOTICE 2014-21 SPECIFICALLY STATES THAT payment made using virtual currency is subject to information reporting. If, in the course of your trade or business, you pay an individual (not a corporation) virtual currency worth $600 or more in a calendar year, you are required to issue that individual Form 1099-MISC (Form 1099-NEC starting in 2020) and send a copy to the IRS. As with everything else in Tax World, the forms are set up to report in dollars; this means that you'll have to determine the dollar value of the virtual currency you paid out as of the date you paid it. And—you guessed it—you must also retain documentation showing how you calculated that amount.

If you are paying interest to someone using virtual currency, then plan on issuing that person a 1099-INT with a copy going to the IRS; again, it's up to you to determine and document the dollar value of the virtual currency that you paid.

Notice 2014-21 specifically states that payment of

virtual currency is subject to what's called "backup with-holding". If you are going to pay someone virtual currency worth $600 or more in a calendar year and that person has refused to give you a tax ID number (social security number, TIN, or EIN), you are required to withhold 24% of that income and send it to the IRS. (You'll have to send it in dollars; the IRS does not yet accept virtual currency as payment for taxes, though several states do.) Failure to send in backup withholding if you are required to do so is penalized.

Again, be proactive. If you plan to pay someone $600 or more in the course of your trade or business, have that person fill out a Form W-9 before you even begin. Pay no attention to the inevitable whining, and don't let them start work—no matter how eager you both are—until that form is completely filled out and signed.

If you are an employer who pays employees in virtual currency, you are responsible for meeting the same payroll reporting requirements as any other employer—you just have to remember to convert the payments of virtual currency into dollars. An employer's failure to file and pay payroll taxes is heavily penalized. These penalties can be levied on the business, the business owner, and any other "responsible parties". I strongly advise you to take payroll reporting and withholding requirements quite seriously.

Reporting requirements are far easier for 1099 workers than for employees but be aware that the distinction between an employee and an independent contractor is a matter of facts and circumstances, not a matter of opinion or preference. There are stiff penalties for treating someone as an independent contractor when they are actually an employee; it's important to know the difference. The distinction between employee and independent contractor is based on three factors: Behavioral, Financial, and Type of Relationship. Read IRS guidance, specifically Publication 15-A, to determine the reality of your own situation and avoid wishful thinking.

Finally, let's not forget that paying your household employee in virtual currency is no different than paying that person in dollars. A household employee can be a housekeeper, maid, nanny, gardener, etc. If you pay any one of these workers $2,100 or more (as of 2019) then you are generally required to withhold Social Security and Medicare tax. Typically, the painter, plumber and handyman are independent contractors, and so you are not responsible for paying their Social Security and Medicare taxes for them.

Failure to file any of the required forms can lead to penalties under IRC §6721, *Failure to file correct information returns* and §6722, *Failure to furnish correct payee statements.*

7
Investing in Virtual Currency

BECAUSE VIRTUAL CURRENCY IS CONSIDERED property, gains and losses that arise from investing in virtual currency must be reported as short-term or long-term gains or losses. The good news is that if you hold virtual currency as an investment for 366 days or more, gains are treated as capital gains and taxed at a favorable rate. That favorable rate can save you thousands of tax dollars.

Short-term gains are taxed as ordinary income. Capital losses can be used to offset capital gains; but, as with stocks or other property, the amount of loss that can be used to offset other types of income is limited to $3,000 per year; the rest is rolled forward and used against future gains. This $3,000 limit was put in place in 1978 and has never been raised. If it *had* been adjusted for inflation, that $3,000 would be $12,000 today. Complain to your Congressperson.

Gain or loss is calculated by subtracting your cost basis from your proceeds. To use a simple example, let's say that in April of 2015 you purchased ten BTC for $236 each, for a total of $2,360. In May of 2019 you decided to sell these ten BTC for $5,000 each, for a total of $50,000. You have a long-term capital gain of $47,640.

Sale price: $50,000
Cost basis: ($2,360)
Gain: $47,640

Now let's add one small wrinkle: transaction fees. You paid fees when you purchased the BTC, so add these fees to the purchase price. If you paid $46 in fees, your cost basis would be $2,360 + $46 = $2406. You paid fees when you sold the BTC. If your fees were $745, your proceeds would be $50,000 – $745 = $49,255. Your gain would be $49,255 – $2,406 = $46,849. Because you held these BTC for more than one year, you would pay tax at the preferred capital gain rate, rather than at the ordinary income rate.

In this example, you knew your cost basis because either a) you kept a record of it, b) you use a wallet that kept a record of it or c) you looked it up online. That's easy enough. Now, let's say you sold those BTC in May of 2019, but have no idea as to when you purchased them or what you paid for them. Without proof of basis, the IRS can choose to assume a worst-case scenario: a basis of zero and a purchase date of less than a year of the sale date. With these worst-case assumptions, you'd pay tax on the entire gain at ordinary income rates. And that would be unfortunate.

Now consider another example: in April of 2015, you bought five BTC for $236 each, for a total of $1,180, and another five BTC in January of 2019 for $3,600 each, for a total of $18,000. In May of 2019, you sold seven BTC for $5,000 each. How would you calculate your gain?

Using the FIFO method, we first sell the BTC that we first purchased back in April of 2015. Let's ignore fees for the moment, just to keep the math easy. If we sell the 5 BTC for $5,000 each, then our proceeds are $25,000. Our cost basis is $1,180. So our capital gain is $25,000 – $1,180 – $23,280. Again, it's considered long-term because you owned those BTC for a year before selling them.

Sale price: $25,000
Cost basis: ($1,180)
Gain: $23,820

But we still have two more BTC to sell, the ones we purchased in January of 2019 for $3,600 each, for a total purchase price of $7,200. We're now selling them for $5,000 each, for a total sale price of $10,000.

Sale price: $10,000
Cost basis: ($7,200)
Gain: $2,800

Because you held these BTC for less than a year, the gain will be taxed as a short-term capital gain, aka ordinary income.

So we have $23,820 in long-term gain and $2,800 in short-term gain.

Incidentally, in Tax World, your holding period actually starts the day *after* you purchased the asset and ends on the day you sell it. If you purchased BTC on April 1st, 2018 and sold those same BTC on April 1st, 2019, that would be short-term gain. If you sold it on April 2nd of 2019, it would be long-term gain. Pay close attention to your holding period.

Now for a tougher example. I've limited the number of digits in the number of BTC purchased and sold to make this easier to follow. I'm more interested in having you understand the logic behind this process than nit-picking the exact dollar amounts.

Assume you have made the following purchases:

Date	BTC	Total Price
Aug. 15, 2015	1.0670	$282.96
Sept. 15, 2015	0.0723	$16.62
Oct. 15, 2015	2.3642	$602.42

And then you have the following sales:

Date	BTC	Total Price
Aug. 15, 2016	0.1034	$37.10
Oct. 15, 2016	1.0000	$399.48
Nov. 15, 2016	1.2777	$909.67

Your thinking should run like this: OK, I sold 0.1034 BTC on August 15, 2016. Which of the BTC did I sell? Meaning: what did I pay for that BTC and when did I purchase it? Using the FIFO method, I sold 0.1034 of the 1.0670 BTC that I purchased back on August 15, 2015. I know I paid $282.96 for 1.0670 BTC, so how much did the 0.1034 BTC cost? If you divide $282.96 by 1.0670, you quickly discover that the per unit BTC price you paid was $265.19 per BTC. Multiplying that by 0.1034 tells you that 0.1034 BTC cost you $27.42. You sold it for $37.10, so you have a gain of $9.68. Since you didn't wait that extra day, this is a short-term gain.

The next step in your thinking should be this: I sold 1.0000 BTC on October 15, 2016. Again, which BTC did I sell? What did I pay for it and when did I purchase it? Using the FIFO method, I have 1.0670 – 0.1034 = 0.9636 BTC left from that August 15, 2015 purchase. I already know that the per unit price for the BTC I purchased on August 15, 2015 was $265.19. Multiplying that by the 0.9636 BTC gives me $255.54. (Note that you get the same result if you take the full purchase price of $282.96 and subtract the $27.42 that you sold in August 2016.) So I sold 0.9636 BTC worth $255.54; the remaining 1.0000 – 0.9636 = 0.0364 BTC that I sold on October 15, 2016 came from the BTC that I purchased on September 15, 2015. How much did that 0.0364 BTC cost me? The unit price of that BTC was $399.48, so the purchase price of the 0.0364 is $399.48 × 0.0364 = $14.54. Total cost basis of the 1.0000 BTC sold is $255.54 + $14.54 = $270.08. Gain is purchase price minus cost basis: $399.48 – $270.08 = $129.40. And, happily, it's all long-term gain.

Next: I sold 1.2777 BTC on November 15, 2016. Which of my BTC did I sell, what did I pay for it and when did I buy it? Well, I've exhausted the batch purchased on August 15, 2015 and I sold 0.0364 of the batch purchased on September 15, 2015, but I've still got 0.0723 – 0.0364 = 0.0359 BTC from that batch. So first I need to sell that. With a unit price of $399.48, the purchase price of 0.0359 was $399.48 × 0.0359 = $14.34. That accounts for 0.0359 of the BTC sold; I still have to account for the remaining 1.2777 – 0.0359 = 1.2416 BTC sold. That all came from the batch I purchased on October 15, 2015. Again, I calculate the unit price of the October batch by dividing $602.42 by 2.3642 = $254.81. I multiply the $254.81 by 1.2416 to get $316.37. Total cost basis of the BTC sold on November 15, 2016 is $14.34 + $316.37 = $330.71. Since the sales proceeds were

$909.67, our gain is $909.67 − $330.71 = $578.96. Again, all long-term gain.

You can see that this gets very complex very quickly. You can do the math by hand, or with Excel or one of its cheaper cousins.

But if the entire above discussion made you feel like you want to pass out OR you are going to have hundreds of transactions, then you need to get help. There are several software companies that will let you import your csv files directly from your exchange and let you print out a transaction summary that you can just hand to your tax advisor. Some of the better-known ones: TokenTax, BearTax, CryptoTrader.tax, ZenLedger, CoinTracker, and Bitcoin. Tax.

Be aware of a few issues: first, exchanges are being created faster than the tax software firms can keep up. If you don't want to play fun-with-spreadsheets, then stick with exchanges that are supported by the software of your choice. Also, many of my clients have experienced significant problems with the results of the importing process; fees may not be accounted for, donations and gifts aren't accounted for, and so on. Don't hesitate to use your own knowledge to correct the information that is printed out. Your tax advisor is going to utilize whatever information you give her; don't expect her to be cognizant of the ins and outs of your transactions.

IMPORTANT NOTE: As of the end of 2019, the IRS published an online page called *Frequently Asked Questions on Virtual Currency Transactions*. This page stated that tax-payers may use a specific identification method, but FIFO is the default inventory method. Note that these FAQs are not considered true guidance, as the IRS can change the FAQs without notice, but it's probably best to comply.

8
Spending Virtual Currency

SINCE VIRTUAL CURRENCY IS CONSIDERED property, every time you spend virtual currency, no matter how small the amount, you have created a taxable transaction. EVERY TIME. As of this writing, the IRS has offered no *de minimis* (this is Latin for "too trivial to be considered"; I use the term because the IRS uses it, not because I want to show off) transaction amount to ease this burden.

This is a serious problem for virtual currency true believers who base their entire financial lives on virtual currency. Every time they buy a cup of coffee with that handy bitcoins-to-dollars debit card, they create a taxable transaction. A better strategy, from the viewpoint of Tax World, would be to periodically convert a larger amount of virtual currency into dollars—perhaps once a week or once a month—thereby limiting the number of transactions you must cope with. I understand that this solution goes against the grain for the true believer but do consider simplifying your life while waiting for the IRS to cut us some slack.

If you are earning virtual currency and don't want to deal with reporting capital gains, the solution is simply to convert your earnings to dollars immediately upon receipt. You'll still have to report the earnings, but you won't have to report a sale every time you convert some virtual currency into dollars.

Alternately, again, consider utilizing one of the newborn csv conversion software platforms available online.

It's worth stressing that just because the reporting is onerous doesn't mean the IRS doesn't require it.

9
Fair Market Value

NOTICE 2014-21 SPECIFICALLY STATES THAT taxpayers must report the fair market value of their virtual currency as of the *date* that the currency was received. Not the time, mind you; the date.

This creates some interesting complications because, as you know, the value of virtual currency fluctuates from minute to minute, so the fair market value may be subject to interpretation. The taxpayer may choose to use the average price on the day of receipt, or the price as of the moment of receipt, or the day's high, or the day's low. And different taxpayers may choose differently; someone paying a worker with virtual currency may choose to use that day's high, while the person receiving the wages may choose to use the day's low. (Though if a 1099 or W-2 has been filed, the worker will probably be stuck with whatever methodology the employer used to create the 1099 or W-2.) And one taxpayer may try using different methods for different occasions; who wouldn't be tempted to go with a higher price when purchasing virtual currency and the lower price when selling it?

However, that fun all came to an end when, in *Frequently Asked Questions on Virtual Currency Transactions*, the online resource the IRS provided in late 2019, the IRS changed their tune and specified date *and time* of receipt. Again, remember that these FAQs are not considered true guidance, but from 2019 and forward, it is likely that the earlier opportunities of timing your income no longer exist.

10
Giving or Donating Virtual Currency

Let's say your favorite charity—any approved 501(c) (3) organization approved by the IRS for tax-deductible donations—is short-sighted and only accepts donations in dollars. So, you sell some virtual currency in order to make a donation, potentially incurring either a capital gain or a capital loss. You then would be allowed to deduct the full fair market value of that donation, plus fees involved in the sale, up to 60% of your adjusted gross income. If you donate more than 60% of your adjusted gross income, you can roll the unused donation amount forward for up to five years.

But perhaps this wonderful charitable organization has a merchant account that allows them to accept virtual currency. In this case, you could donate actual virtual currency as PROPERTY. This means that if you had held that virtual currency for one year plus one day or longer, you get to deduct the fair market value of that currency as of the date of the donation, without having to cash it in and pay the capital gains tax. If you donate property that has been held for less than one year and one day, you only get to deduct what you paid for it.

When donating property, you are only allowed to deduct up to 60% of your adjusted gross income; again, any remaining deduction rolls forward for up to five years. Note that this 60% limitation is only 30% for appreciated securities; since virtual currencies has been defined as property rather than securities, it is my belief that virtual currency donations are not limited to 30%.

Be aware, also, that there are reporting requirements involved in the donation of property. If you donate property valued at more than $500, you are required to include Form 8283 with your tax return; it makes sense to assume that this same requirement holds true for virtual currency.

However, if you donate property worth more than $5,000, the IRS rule is that you must get an appraisal of the property (which you must send in with your tax return) and a written and signed acknowledgement from the charity stating the value of the property you donated. There's an exception for this get-an-appraisal requirement for donations of publicly traded stock, since the value of stock is available on the stock exchange. While it seems unfair that virtual currency doesn't merit a similar exception—given that the fair market value of pretty much any such currency is available on any blockchain explorer, we don't yet have IRS guidance allowing this. Your best bet at this point is to keep your donations under the $5,000 mark.

Remember that charitable donations are itemized deductions; making the donations helps you from a tax standpoint only if you itemize deductions. This is true even if you are a small business filing a Schedule C or filing as an S Corporation. Donations do not reduce the taxable income of the business; they flow over to Schedule A as itemized deductions. If the taxpayer doesn't itemize, then there is no tax benefit to the donation. (A discussion of the karmic benefits of the donation is beyond the scope of this book.)

Then there are those donations that are not tax-deductible. When you give virtual currency to a person or organization that is not a 501(c) (3) organization, you have made a gift, not a donation. No worries for you; as long as you don't give any single person/organization more than $15,000 (as of 2019), you have no reporting obligations whatsoever.

11
Inheriting Virtual Currency

SINCE VIRTUAL CURRENCY IS PROPERTY, it seems reasonable to apply property inheritance rules to virtual currency. And this is entirely good news.

When someone dies, their property generally passes to their beneficiaries with a tax basis equal to the fair market value of that property upon the date of the death, or at an alternate valuation date (exactly six months after death) if the estate executor so chooses. A taxpayer who bought virtual currency when it was inexpensive can pass that currency on to his or her heirs and entirely avoid capital gains tax. But read the fine print: if the heirs are cunning and give their virtual currency to dear old dad less than a year before his death with the idea of getting it back with a fair market value basis, they will be in for a surprise: the IRS wasn't born yesterday. The heirs will get that currency back with an adjusted basis equal to dear old dad's adjusted basis at the time of his death, aka what those heirs originally paid for it. The benefit of stepped-up basis is not available in this situation. Further discussion regarding the adjusted basis of gifted assets is beyond the scope of this book: talk to your tax advisor.

If you inherit virtual currency, document its fair market value as of the date of the decedent's death. If you sell it immediately, you must report the sale, but should incur no taxable gain; you may, in fact, sustain a deductible loss because of the selling fees.

12
Losses of Virtual Currency

IF YOUR VIRTUAL CURRENCY HAS been lost or stolen, or has vanished in a defunct exchange, the IRS provides us with very little guidance—actually, no guidance—as to how to handle this on your tax return.

Prior to the Tax Cuts and Jobs Act of late 2017, such a loss would have been reported as a Casualty and Theft Loss on Schedule A. Unfortunately, that category of deductions was killed by the Tax Cuts & Jobs Act. So—now what?

We do know that if you have a security that becomes worthless, IRC §165 permits you to take a capital loss on Form 8949, which flows over to Schedule D. The amount of the loss is the taxpayer's basis in the stock minus any amounts recovered. Note that regardless of when during the year the stock officially becomes worthless, the final day of the holding period is always December 31st of that tax year, increasing the odds that this loss will be long-term rather than short-term. The loss is allowed only if there is no reasonable chance of recovery. If the chance of recovery is not yet known, then the deduction must wait until the tax year in which the loss can be confirmed.

Can Form 8949 be used to report the theft or loss of virtual currency? The instructions for the Form state that the form is to be used to report:

Sales and exchanges of capital assets

- Gains from involuntary conversions other than from casualty or theft of capital assets not used in trade or business
- Non-business bad debts
- Worthlessness of a security
- And a couple of things pertaining to Qualified Opportunity Funds that we don't care about here.

Loss due to theft or hacking isn't a sale or exchange of capital assets, so that's out. Number 2 looks promising until you actually read it—right, gains not losses and from involuntary conversions other than casualty and theft. So there goes that possibility. It isn't a bad debt. And it isn't a security. And it isn't a Qualified Opportunity Fund.

OK, so now what?

Another possibility is Form 4797, Sales of Business Property. This is the form you use to report the abandonment of property. To establish that property was abandoned, the taxpayer must establish the following:

1. The loss was incurred in a profit-motive activity. (That should be easy to establish.)

2. The taxpayer can show intent to abandon. (While this has not yet been tested in a crypto situation, but it has been established in the past that deciding that if efforts to recover possession of an asset would be futile, then that constitutes abandonment. I do see some possibility here. If my exchange got hacked, then yes, I could go hire a bunch of software geniuses to try to recover my lost currency, but it probably isn't worth it given the cost of software geniuses and the likelihood of failure, so I'm abandoning it.)

3. Abandonment did not involve any consideration. (This means that no money was received, and this is easy because if there was consideration, then we would call it a sale and we'd be back to Form 8949

4. The abandoned asset is not one described in IRC Section 1234A. (This section describes assets such as rights or obligations with respect to property and a section 1256 contract and the idea here is to make sure that cancellation, lapse, expiration or other termination of a right or obligation be treated as a capital gain or loss rather than abandonment.)

Personally, I like the Form 4797 concept because losses due to abandonment are ordinary losses, not capital losses! Which means you can take the entire amount of the loss in the year the loss occurs; you aren't limited to the $3,000 per year that you're permitted if it is a capital loss.

However, and this can't be over-emphasized, there is no precedent for Form 8949 or Form 4797 at this point. This is a loss you take entirely at your own risk. Consider hiring a tax attorney to help. If the loss doesn't warrant the expense of an attorney, you might want to skip it entirely and not risk being The Court Case that ends up deciding the issue for everyone else.

I'd advise against taking a loss if there is no documentation showing the basis of the lost property and the loss itself; I'd also advise against it if the loss was due to the taxpayer's carelessness or stupidity.

If you do decide to take a loss, remember that the most you can deduct is your original basis (aka what you paid for it plus fees). You have a loss equivalent to your original investment. If the currency was worth more than what you paid for it at the time of the loss, too bad for you; you still only get to deduct what you paid for it.

What about losses of virtual currency that you weren't holding as an investment, but perhaps loaned to a friend? Let's say you loaned 3 BTC to your buddy. It was just a friendly loan, no paperwork, no interest rate, and Buddy vanished, taking the private keys to your BTC with him. Guess what? No help from Tax World. You've got no paper trail, nothing to substantiate your claim that this was a loan and not a gift.

Having wised up, when you loan Sally 2 BTC the following year, you have her sign paperwork stating the terms of repayment, including an interest rate. Alas, Sally suddenly stops answering her phone. You send certified letters (keeping copies), you take her to small claims court (she doesn't show up). Under these circumstances, you've probably got a good claim to a non-business bad debt, which you can take as a short-term capital loss. (Yes, even if these legal shenanigans went on for more than a year, non-business bad debts are always short-term.)

If Sally manages to repay 1 BTC, you can still take a loss for the remaining BTC. If you've already taken the deduction when she pays you, then you have to report the fair market value of the collected BTC as ordinary income.

Note that losses on virtual currency are the sort of thing the IRS will probably enjoy auditing; make sure your documentation ducks are all in a row. What did you spend on Worthless Token? Did you remember to report a gain or loss when you "traded" BTC or Ether in order to obtain Worthless, in case that comes up? We know you don't have a broker's report, but do you at least have printouts detailing your transactions? Screen shots? And if you do take a capital loss in this situation, it's probably a good idea to disclose it in a written statement on the tax return.

13
Wash Sales

A **WASH SALE IS A** situation in which a taxpayer sells a security to reap a tax loss and then immediately buys it again at that reduced price. For example, you buy Stock ABC when it's $1,000 a share. It drops to $50 a share, but you are ever hopeful and think it's going to regain its value. You sell it on December 30th at $50 a share, report a tax loss of $1,000 – $50 = $950. Then on January 10th, you sneakily buy Stock ABC back at $50 a share. Nice try; but, again, the IRS wasn't born yesterday. Anytime a security is purchased within 30 days of a "substantially identical" security being sold at a loss, that loss is disallowed.

It's a fair question to wonder if investors in virtual currency will be held to wash sale rules. The IRS Code in question (§1091) specifically refers to shares of stock or securities, so it's hard to see how the rules applying to wash sales would affect virtual currency without the IRS providing some substantive guidance to that effect.

At this point, it seems reasonable to suppose that virtual currency investors are exempt from wash sale rules.

14
Section 1031 Exchanges

A §1031 EXCHANGE IS A series of transactions that allow for the disposal of one asset and the acquisition of a replacement asset without generating a tax liability until the final asset is sold. Up until the passing of the 2017 Tax Cuts and Jobs Act, the words "like-kind exchange" were bandied about quite freely in virtual currency circles when discussing the tax implications of trading one sort of virtual currency for another. It was assumed by many virtual currency users and investors that the IRS would allow the application of Section 1031 exchanges to trading of virtual currency, so—the theory went—you did not need to report any income if you had simply traded one type of currency for another.

However, the 2017 Tax Cuts and Jobs Act put a lid on the whole thing by declaring that like-kind exchanges would hereafter be restricted to real estate. This means that there is no option for utilizing like-kind exchange to defer taxation on virtual currency trades for 2018 and later.

Here's how so-called trading is going to work from here on out: when you trade one virtual currency for another, you have effectively sold the original virtual currency at its fair market value (thus creating a taxable transaction) and purchased the second virtual currency with the proceeds. The second currency has a cost basis equivalent to the fair market value of the first currency at the time of the trade. Example: let's say you buy one BTC for $265.19 and about six months later, you trade the BTC for some quantity of Ethereum. And let's say that on the day you trade it, the BTC is worth $310.10. You have, effectively, sold that BTC and have a reportable gain of $310.10 – $265.19 = $44.91. Your Ethereum now has a cost basis of $310.10.

However, it is possible that like-kind exchange is still an option for 2017 and earlier tax returns. Note that to utilize a like-kind exchange, you must file Form 8824 with your tax return in the year of the exchange. Form 8824 will give the IRS details about the exchange. If you didn't file Form 8824 when you filed the return, then you didn't have a like-kind exchange; that tax return should possibly be amended to include Form 8824 for every trade you want considered like-kind, or to report those trades as sales instead. Note, as always, that I am giving you the law of Tax World and not commenting on the likelihood of you being caught.

15
Other Reporting Options

BACK IN CHAPTER 6, I went through a sample sale situation using FIFO, and I mentioned that in December of 2019, the IRS created a page called *Frequently Asked Questions on Virtual Currency*. One of the questions specifically asked if a taxpayer could select which units of currency are deemed sold, exchanged or otherwise disposed of, and the answer was yes.

The IRS then specified that such identification required documenting "the specific unit's unique digital identifier such as a private key, public key, and address, or by records showing the transaction information for all units of a specific virtual currency, such as Bitcoin, held in a single account, wallet, or address. This information must show (1) the date and time each unit was acquired, (2) your basis and the fair market value of each unit at the time it was acquired, (3) the date and time each unit was sold, exchanged, or otherwise disposed of, and (4) the fair market value of each unit when sold, exchanged, or disposed of, and the amount of money or the value of property received for each unit."

The FAQs then go on to state that if the taxpayer does not specifically identify used disposed of, then the default methodology would be FIFO.

Most virtual currency platforms are offering both FIFO and the specific identification method are options; just remember that all of this could change tomorrow.

16
Foreign Reporting Requirements

TAXPAYERS WHO HAVE A FINANCIAL interest in or signature authority over foreign financial accounts are required to file Report of Foreign Bank and Financial Accounts (FBAR) with the Financial Crimes Enforcement Network (FinCEN) if the aggregate value of those accounts exceeds $10,000 at any time during the calendar year. So, does that mean that holding virtual currency in a foreign exchange requires the filing of an FBAR if the value of that account exceed $10,000 at any point during the year?

At the end of 2019, the American Institute of Certified Public Accountants reached out—again—to the Treasury Department's Financial Crimes Enforcement Network (aka FinCEN) and this time actually, miraculously, got an answer. The Treasury Department responded that as of right now, virtual currency is not considered to be held in an offshore account. That means that currently, you do not need to report cryptocurrency on an FBAR.

So hooray for that. But wait—what about Form 8938,

Statement of Specified Foreign Financial Assets? Form 8938 has a much broader application than the FBAR. You are supposed to file Form 8938 if the total value of your foreign financial assets exceed certain dollar amounts during the year or at year end.

These amounts are as follows: For single filers, the form must be filed if the market value of your foreign assets is at least $50K on December 31st, or $75K at any time during the year. For married filing jointly filers, the form must be filed if the market value of your foreign assets is at least $100K on December 31st, or $150K at any time during the year.

Are we required to file Form 8938 for crypto? Guess what? Surprise—no one knows. You would think that if the Treasury Department says that crypto isn't considered as being held offshore, this would be an obvious NO. Apparently, though, an IRS official was asked if the IRS will assess penalties against taxpayers who haven't been disclosing digital assets on Form 8938, and the official responded: if taxpayers had been reporting taxable cryptocurrency transactions on their returns during prior years and properly filed Form 8938 going forward, the IRS probably would not pursue them for prior tax years. This seems a little passive aggressive given that the IRS has issued no guidance at all on this subject.

17
Initial Coin Offerings

INITIAL COIN OFFERINGS (ICOs) ARE the virtual version of IPOs, or initial public offerings. An ICO is faster and cheaper than an IPO and can be incredibly profitable for issuers.

Via an ICO, a new digital currency is created and sold online, sometimes raising tens of millions of dollars in just minutes. The idea is that this new currency will become the latest virtual currency of choice or will be redeemable for services such as data storage. Just as with IPOs, the investor is hoping to buy in cheap at the starting gate and reap the gains as it appreciates over time.

We're talking about some serious money. Here's how much money was raised by these ICOs:

EOS: $4.1B
Telegram: $1.7B
Dragon: $320M
Huobi: $300M

Hdac: $258M
Filecoin: $257M
Tezos: $232M
Sirin Labs: $157.9M
Bancor: $152M
Etc.

The number of dollars raised by ICOs in the first quarter of 2018 surpassed all the dollars raised in 2017. However, it does seem to be slowing down in 2019; only $118M was raised in the first quarter of 2019.

The Securities and Exchange Commission (SEC) has gotten pretty interested in ICOs. In August of 2018 the SEC published a paper stating that ICOs may qualify as an offering of a security, subject to the federal regulations that apply to securities.

"As a general matter, though, ICOs are more likely to qualify as offerings of 'securities' when token purchasers (1) are motivated primarily by a desire for financial returns (as opposed to a desire to use or consume some good or service for which tokens can be exchanged), and (2) lack a meaningful ability to control the activities on which their profits will depend."

The SEC has gotten involved, resulting in hundreds of startups having their virtual hands slapped for violating securities law and then quietly—or not quietly—agreeing to refund investors' money and pay fines.

You can see how interesting this is: virtual currencies are considered property per the IRS, but potential securities to the SEC. Again, we're in new territory here, where old definitions don't work.

Payment for an ICO currency is usually made in an established virtual currency such as BTC or Ethereum. Your basis in the new coins is equal to your basis in the virtual currency with which you purchased those new coins; if you spent $10,000 worth of Bitcoin to buy AmyCoin, then your basis in the AmyCoin is $10,000. And don't forget that you now have a taxable event; you have essentially sold that $10,000 Bitcoin and you may therefore have a gain or a loss, depending on your basis in that Bitcoin.

As ever, record-keeping is essential.

18
Tokens, Air Drops, and Forks

THERE'S SOME CONFUSION ABOUT WHAT constitutes a token and what constitutes a coin. From a technical standpoint (not that these things matter in Tax World), a token is built on top of an existing blockchain, while a coin has its own blockchain.

It's probably a gross generalization to say that coins are meant to be a unit of value and exchange, while a token represents an asset or access to an asset . . . but that does seem to be the common trend. A token may be used to purchase goods on a certain site; Musicoin, for example, is a token that allows its owners to access items on the Musicoin platform. A token might also represent loyalty points.

How we handle tokens in Tax World is probably just a question of how it was obtained. In theory, if the token was purchased, then it has a fair market value; there will be gain or loss upon the ultimate sale or exchange of that token. If the token was given out for free and it has a fair market value, it's possible that this should be treated as an airdrop, thereby incurring a taxable gain. Notice 2019-24 did not address tokens, but you can see the similarity in principle. There can't be a loss, as the basis is zero. In most cases, however, there will be neither gain nor loss on these tokens, and thus nothing to track. Stay tuned, though: things change very fast in virtual currency.

An airdrop is the free distribution of virtual currency to community members. To receive the gift, you might need to hold some minimum number of coins or perhaps perform a small task.

And then there are forks. A fork represents a change to the blockchain protocol. There are hard forks and soft forks. A hard fork is a change that renders older versions of that protocol invalid; think of it as a software upgrade that isn't compatible with previous versions of the software. All users must upgrade to the new software. A soft fork is a software upgrade that is compatible with earlier versions. In Tax World, though, we don't care all that much about what happened to the software and more about the financial result of the fork, because a hard fork will often result in free coins being distributed.

When you receive an airdrop, or when you receive some currency because your currency forked, per Notice 2019-24, you have ordinary income as of the date that this new currency is available to you, calculated at the fair market value of that currency as of the date of availability. Note that if it is promised to you, but you cannot yet access it, you do not yet have income. It's income only as of the date that you can access it in order to sell it, trade it, whatever.

19
Virtual Currency IRAs

YES, THERE ARE IRAs THAT will let you invest in virtual currency. These are just like any other IRA accounts, subject to the same income restrictions and requirements. You don't even have to tell your tax preparer that you've investing in virtual currency; just make sure you understand whether that IRA contribution will help your tax situation (deductible) or not (nondeductible). Your tax advisor can help you.

20
Loaning Virtual Currency

A NEW WRINKLE IN THE virtual currency world is loaning virtual currency and receiving "interest" while the virtual currency is held.

I put the word "interest" in quotes because it isn't clear if these payments are actually interest in the true sense of the word. If virtual currency is property and you are allowing someone to use that property for some period of time, might it be that the payments are actually rent rather than interest?

Interest is reported on Schedule B; rent is reported on Schedule E. Probably the best bet is to comply with whatever documentation was sent to the IRS; if a 1099-INT was filed, then report it as interest. If a 1099-MISC was filed, then enter the income in accordance with whichever box was used in the 1099. If there was no reporting—surprise—you might avoid the question as to what type of income it is by reporting it on the "Other Income" line of the 1040.

If you are receiving this income in dollars, then that's what you report; if you are receiving it in virtual currency, then your income is the fair market value of those coins on the date of receipt. Those reported amounts then become the basis of those coins when you eventually sell them; the holding period begins on the date of receipt.

21

1099-K

FORM 1099-K IS USED TO report payments received through payment card transactions and settlement of third-party payment network transactions. Note that this is about you *receiving* money via credit cards or a payment network, not about you *spending* money via credit cards or a payment network.

Why is this a big deal in virtual currency?

Simply because if you sell virtual currency on an exchange then it's possible that you and the IRS will receive a 1099-K from that exchange. The IRS requires that a third party submit a 1099-K for a customer if that third party has processed over 200 transactions and paid out over $20,000 over the course of a year for that customer.

There are two interesting issues in connection with receiving a 1099-K from an exchange. First, you'll note that it shows money received, but not money spent. For example, you may have received $250,000 in virtual credit sales but you may have spent $300,000 buying that virtual currency in the first place. The $250,000 will show up; the $300,000 will not. The IRS is going to assume that you have $250,000 of income and it's up to you to prove that you don't.

The second interesting issue is this: where do you report that 1099-K number on your tax return? Remember that the IRS' matching program is going to be looking for that gross amount somewhere on the tax return; if it doesn't see it, you'll get a letter from the IRS telling you what the tax is on that $250,000 and requesting payment. So that gross number needs to show up somewhere.

Typically, a 1099-K is issued in conjunction with business income; the matching program may be specifically looking for that number on a Schedule C. If you instead put that gross number on a Form 8949 and thus a Schedule D, then subtract out the basis of those sales, will the matching program be satisfied? We don't know.

22
The IRS is Serious

MAKE NO MISTAKE, THE IRS is deeply interested in virtual currency income reporting. Though we are nowhere near the gold rush of 2017, there is still a lot of money being made in crypto and the IRS wants a piece of the action.

The problem the IRS has is this: other than the 1099K, there is not a lot of reporting going on. Imagine if the IRS had to rely on taxpayer honesty when it came to interest, dividends, and stock sales! That's pretty much the position the IRS is in.

The IRS has made several efforts at getting taxpayers to report virtual currency income. One of the most famous—or infamous—of these was the 2016 John Doe Summons to Coinbase. A John Doe Summons is a specific right given to the IRS regarding an investigation of a specific, unidentified person or group of persons. This is different from a normal summons, where the person being investigated is actually named. Coinbase, of course, said absolutely not, we are not complying with this. And the matter went to court.

Time passed. The entire virtual currency community held its collective breath during this process, as you might imagine, absolutely terrified that they would be outed by Coinbase. In November 2017, a full year after it all started, a California federal court ordered Coinbase to turn over identifying records just for users who had transactions of $20K or more in any single year between 2013 and 2015. Coinbase estimated that about 14,000 users would fit into that category.

In 2018, the IRS announced the approval of five compliance campaigns, one of which was virtual currency.

In the summer of 2019, the IRS sent out three different versions of what they called a Virtual Currency Letter: Form 6173, Form 6174 and Form 6174-A. These letters basically said that the IRS has an eye on you and you better be correctly reporting your virtual currency activities. If you haven't done so, you better file an amendment. And yes, these letters did indeed strike some fear in the hearts of many.

And in 2020, our 2019 1040s included the famous Crypto Question: "At any time during 2019, did you receive, sell, send, exchange, or otherwise acquire any financial interest in any virtual currency?"

If you think the IRS isn't interested in your virtual currency, think again. They are deeply, deeply interested.

23
Audits

THE IRS REQUIRES THAT ALL income, including virtual currency income and gains upon sale, be reported on the tax return for the year in which the income was received. The IRS further expects that documentation supporting the numbers on the tax return will be available for review upon request.

That said, it's been almost pathetically easy to get away with not paying taxes on income derived from virtual currency. This fact isn't lost on the IRS. The Service is starting to get very interested in taxpayers who earn/utilize/spend/ invest in virtual currency, as was evidenced by recent actions against Coinbase. While that legal action didn't pan out quite as the IRS had hoped, it's truly just a matter of time until the legal tangles are untangled and the IRS gets its hands on a whole lot of data that will affect a whole lot of people. When that happens, those people are going to do a whole lot of scrambling to amend tax returns. My advice is to accept the inevitable and start reporting your income immediately. If you don't understand how to do this yourself, get help. "I didn't understand" is not, has never been, and will never be something the IRS is interested in hearing.

Remember that the IRS guidance issued in 2014 was retroactive, as are most of the IRS' pronouncements. If you had virtual currency income at any point, before or after 2014, and you didn't report it, it would be a good idea to amend those returns. Under normal circumstances, the IRS has only three years to audit you; but there are special cases that can extend that time period. If you omitted more than 25% of your income, those three years become six years. And if you have committed tax fraud, there is no time limit. Read that again: NO TIME LIMIT. You'll be hiding under the bed for the rest of your life.

Don't count on the much-vaunted anonymity of virtual currency. While it may be possible for some very savvy trader to remain anonymous, this isn't an option for the average user of virtual currency who utilizes an exchange. Your identity is tied to your account by virtue of email contact and bank or credit card information. Once the IRS can identify a virtual currency account as belonging to an individual, they can extract every transaction from the blockchain.

Furthermore, the IRS does indeed have the resources to engage in the sort of complex data analysis required to track down the owners of the accounts and unravel the blockchain. They'll be aided by tax whistleblowers who receive compensation for providing information that helps the IRS track down virtual currency accounts and owners. If you've received Letter 6174 or 6174-A and are current on your virtual currency filings, you have nothing to worry about; no response is required. Letter 6173 is a more serious matter and requires a response.

Your failure to report all your income can lead to nasty accuracy-related penalties or worse. If the IRS decides that you've willfully engaged in tax fraud, it could decide that your case should be handled by the Criminal Investigation branch of the Service. It is not impossible for a careless virtual currency user to face felony tax evasion charges and a federal prison sentence.

Be aware that if your past virtual currency dealings create the potential for criminal charges, you need to speak with a tax attorney, not an Enrolled Agent or CPA. Only an actual attorney enjoys attorney-client privilege. Unless hired by a tax attorney under a Kovel agreement, an Enrolled Agent or CPA can be subpoenaed by the IRS and become a witness against you.

24
Best Practices for Virtual Currency Taxpayers

I OFFER THE FOLLOWING LIST of "Best Practices" for virtual currency users who would like to avoid problems with the IRS:

1. Given the severity of the possible consequences, getting professional help really is the sensible choice. Don't rely on the nonsense that's passed around on crypto blogs. Find a tax preparer who has experience working with virtual currency taxation and get on their client list. The best time to find your new tax preparer is not—repeat, NOT—during tax season. (We're kind of busy then.)

2. Make sure you know the basis of all virtual currency you own. Document how you arrived at that basis. Use that basis moving forward. This isn't perfect, but it's better than trying to figure it out years from now during a high-pressure audit.

3. If you can't maintain your own spreadsheets, stay with exchanges supported by Bitcoin.tax or similar software. We don't know for certain if the IRS will accept the conclusions drawn by this type of software, but you'll at least be demonstrating that you tried your best to report your income correctly.

4. Print out statements regularly; otherwise, if your exchange shuts down or your computer gets stolen, you'll have proof of NOTHING. If you don't like paper, then scan the report into a safe drive and then shred the paper. Document, document, document. If you can't document it, don't do it.

5. Separate your investment accounts from your personal use accounts. This makes it more likely that the IRS will allow you to take a loss on the investment account.

6. Recognize that tax law for virtual currency is in its infancy. We're all doing our best with very limited information. No one can predict the future of tax law—not even a highly trained and extremely intelligent Enrolled Agent.

25
Best Practices for Tax Preparers

OK, **FELLOW TAX PREPARERS,** this is for you.

1. Include a question about virtual currency use in your standard engagement letter. You may be surprised to discover how many of your clients are dabbling in virtual currency.

2. Create an additional engagement letter for your virtual currency clients to sign. The engagement letter should inform the client that virtual currency tax law is in its infancy and subject to change and that the client is responsible for the accuracy of the data they provide. The engagement letter should specifically ask what activities the client is engaged in: earning, investing, trading, gifting, etc.

3. Spend some time with the client to make sure she understands her tax obligations relative to virtual currency. As has been mentioned, there is a lot of false information out

in the blogs. (My latest favorite: you can save tax money if you trade through an LLC rather than as an individual. Ha.)

4. Unless you are comfortable with the client's level of expertise in preparing the data, have the client utilize a software platform that creates a summary (Form 8949 or .csv file) for you to use in preparing the return.

5. If your client has inherited any virtual currency during the tax year, make sure she documents its fair market value ASAP.

6. Remember that it is still incumbent upon you, if you are a Circular 230 practitioner, to ask questions. How did the client obtain this information? Were all files exported to the software? Etc.

7. Don't take risks for the client; your license is more important than saving the client a bit of tax money. (And remember that the client will throw you under the bus in a heartbeat if the IRS starts asking questions.)

Disclaimer

I said it before, but for those who weren't listening: *this booklet is intended as a general commentary on virtual currency taxation. It is not intended to represent tax law, nor is it intended to apply to any reader's particular tax situation. It is no substitute for the advice of your own tax professional. As an IRS Circular 230 practitioner, I have no responsibility for any positions you take on your tax return, unless I have prepared and signed that tax return. For a detailed analysis of your tax situation, please consult your tax advisor.*

Remember that the tax law which applies to virtual currency is in its early stages, and future alterations are likely. As with virtual currency in general, you proceed at your own risk. The author owns some virtual currency, but has no vested interest in any particular platform, currency, or corporation.

If you need assistance with virtual currency taxes, you can contact me directly (not during tax season) at amy@tucsontaxteam.com. I work with virtual currency users and tax practitioners all over the country.

Made in the USA
Monee, IL
17 July 2021

73784257R00066